HELEN KELLER AND HER MIRACLE WORKER

BIOGRAPHY 3RD GRADE

CHILDREN'S BIOGRAPHY BOOKS

BABY PROFESSOR

EDUCATION KIDS

Speedy Publishing LLC

40 E. Main St. #1156

Newark, DE 19711

www.speedypublishing.com

Copyright 2017

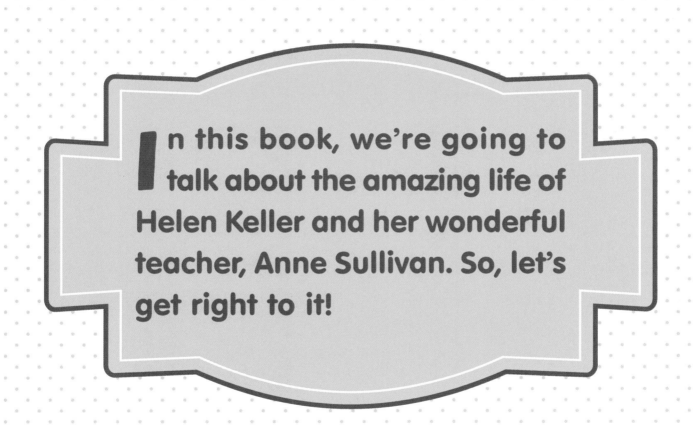

In this book, we're going to talk about the amazing life of Helen Keller and her wonderful teacher, Anne Sullivan. So, let's get right to it!

HELEN KELLER

WHO WAS HELEN KELLER?

As a young child, Helen Keller contracted some type of brain fever and she lost her ability to see as well as her ability to hear. With the help of an amazing teacher, named Anne Sullivan, Helen learned to communicate.

Helen was able to get an education and graduate from college. She went on to become an educator as well as one of the founders of the American Civil Liberties Union.

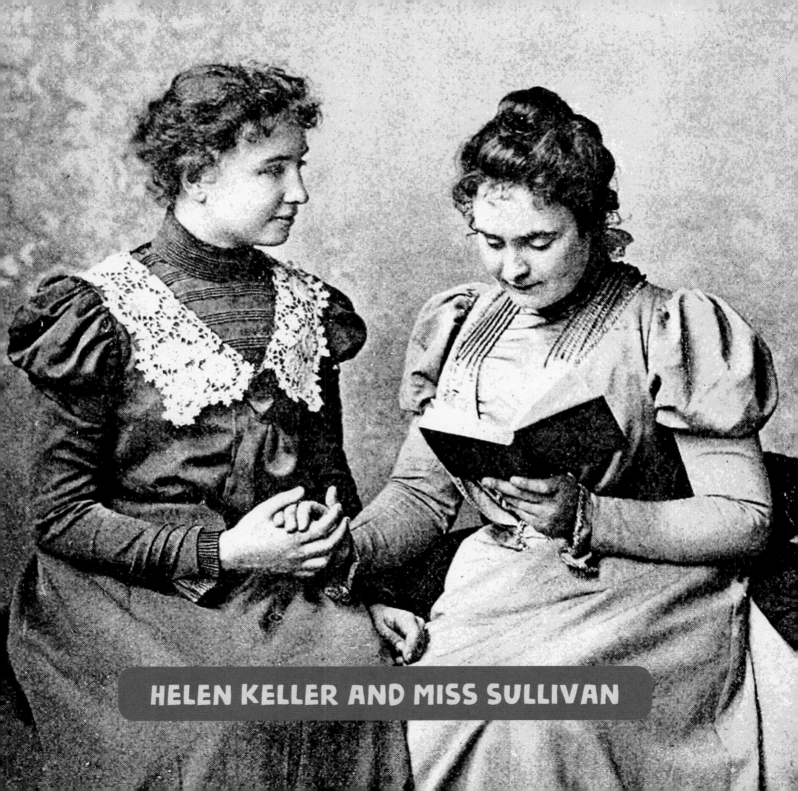

HELEN KELLER AND MISS SULLIVAN

HELEN'S EARLY LIFE

Helen's father, Arthur H. Keller, was a former officer in the Confederate Army during the Civil War. Later in his career, her father was the editor of the North Alabamian, which was a weekly newspaper.

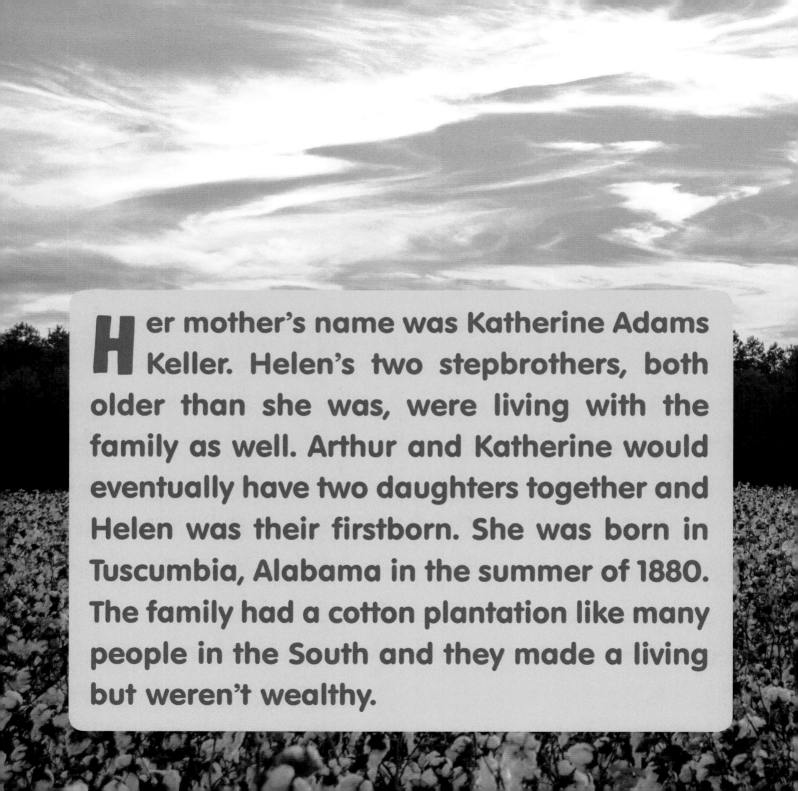

Her mother's name was Katherine Adams Keller. Helen's two stepbrothers, both older than she was, were living with the family as well. Arthur and Katherine would eventually have two daughters together and Helen was their firstborn. She was born in Tuscumbia, Alabama in the summer of 1880. The family had a cotton plantation like many people in the South and they made a living but weren't wealthy.

COTTON FIELD

Helen was very intelligent. She started to talk when she was only 6 months of age and walk around her first birthday. However, a terrible tragedy happened that changed Helen's life forever when she was around a year and a half old.

HELEN LOSES HER SIGHT AND HER HEARING

As a toddler, Helen became very ill with a very high temperature. The doctor said she had a "brain fever." No one knows for sure, but it could have been meningitis, which is caused by an infection in the brain and spinal cord.

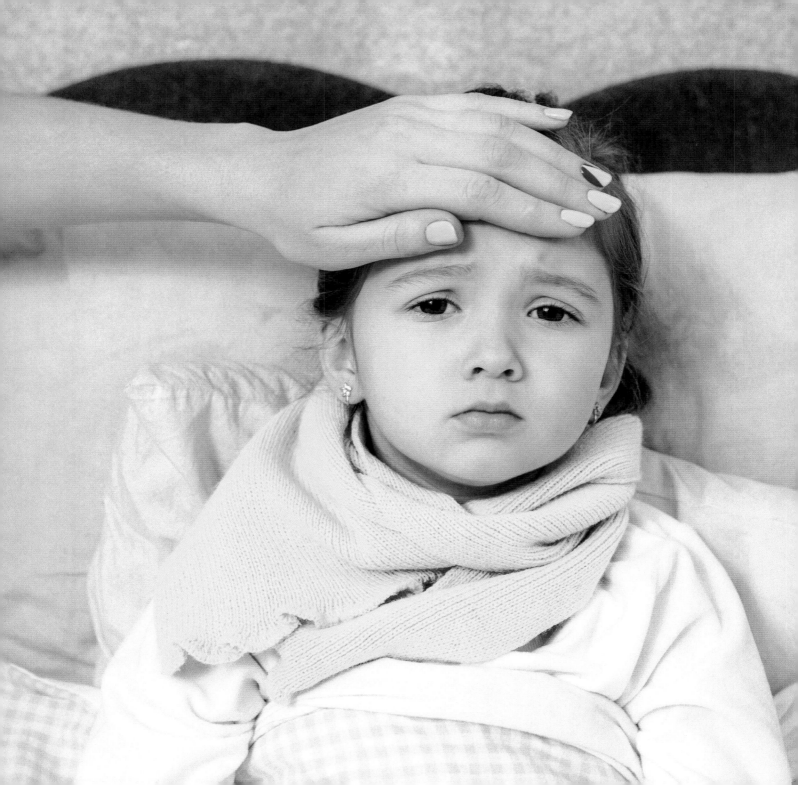

DOCTOR CHECKING GIRL'S EAR

Helen survived the very hot fever, but a few days after her fever went away, her mother noticed something terrifying. Helen showed no reaction when the dinner bell was sounded. When her mother waved a hand in front of her eyes, once again, Helen didn't react at all. She had lost the ability to see or hear.

The family cook had a young daughter and Helen became friends with her. In order to communicate with each other, the young girls invented a secret sign language. By the time Helen was seven years old, they had created over 50 words so they could relay messages to each other.

GIRL USING SIGN LANGUAGE

GIRLS LAUGHING

Helen had become unruly and wild though. She would have a complete temper tantrum when she was angry or upset. When she was in a good mood, she would sometimes giggle for hours on end. She was so out of control that her parents didn't know what to do. Many of her parents' relatives tried to get the family to put Helen in an institution.

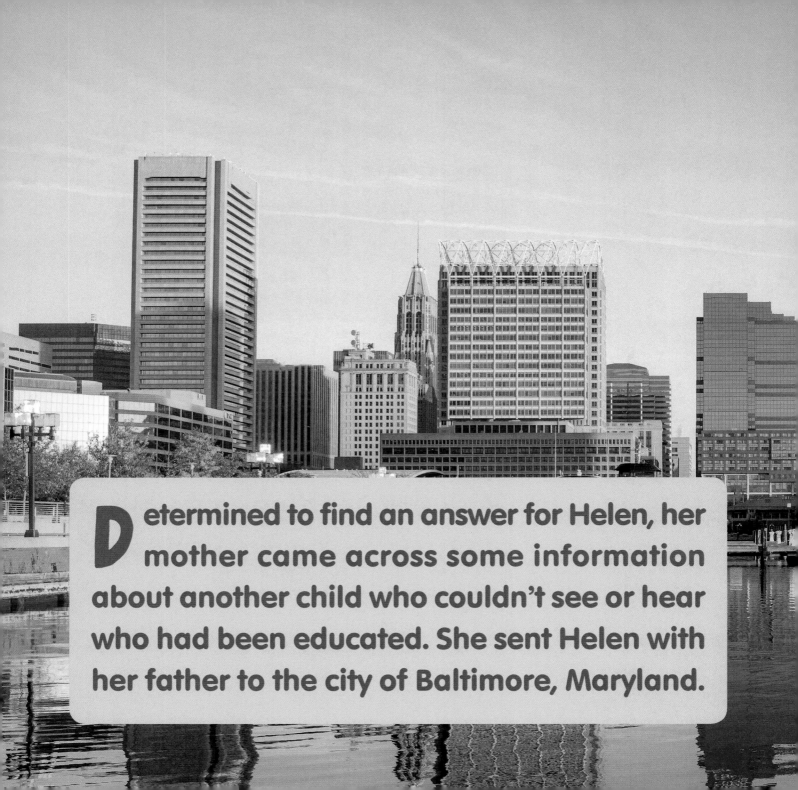

Determined to find an answer for Helen, her mother came across some information about another child who couldn't see or hear who had been educated. She sent Helen with her father to the city of Baltimore, Maryland.

BALTIMORE MARYLAND USA

ALEXANDER GRAHAM BELL

While there, they met with Dr. J. Julian Chisolm, who examined Helen and recommended that her father meet with the famous inventor of the telephone, Alexander Graham Bell.

CHARLES C. PERKINS SCHOOL

When Bell met with them, he recommended that they go to the Perkins Institute, which was a school for the blind located in Boston. The school's director matched them with a brilliant young teacher by the name of Anne Sullivan. Little did they know that Anne would be part of Helen's life for the next 49 years.

THE MIRACLE WORKER ARRIVES

As soon as Anne arrived at the Keller's plantation in the spring of 1887 she went to work. She started by bringing Helen a doll for a gift and then continuously fingering the letters for doll. But, Helen didn't get the connection for quite some time.

At the beginning, she was curious, but as Anne persisted, Helen began to go into violent temper tantrums. She wouldn't cooperate. Even on days when she did try, Anne could tell that Helen didn't understand that the letters her teacher was motioning in the palm of her hand had anything to do with the things she was touching. Anne kept trying, even though it was frustrating that she wasn't getting through to Helen.

GIRL HAVING A TEMPER TANTRUM

COTTAGE

Helen's tantrums got worse and worse. Anne strongly requested that she be allowed to live separately with Helen so that Helen would concentrate and not be distracted by what was happening in the main house. It was difficult for Helen's parents to say yes to this, but they could tell that Anne had Helen's best interests at heart so they agreed. Helen and her teacher moved to a cottage on the property so that Anne could keep Helen's tantrums under control and teach her.

THE BREAKTHROUGH HAPPENS

After many months of doing this, the breakthrough happened. Anne was struggling with Helen and trying to teach her the word "W-A-T-E-R" at the outdoor water pump. She put Helen's hand directly under the spout. As Anne pumped the cool water to flow over Helen's hand, she began to sign the letters for water in Helen's other hand.

GIRL PLAYING WITH THE WATER PUMP

WOMAN TEACHING SIGN LANGUAGE

In that moment, Helen understood and then she signed the word back into her teacher's hand. Then, she pounded on the ground, demanding to know the word from Anne. Anne quickly signed the word for "ground." Helen was filled with excitement. She began running to other objects one by one and getting Anne to give her the sign names for them. By the end of that day, her miracle worker teacher had taught Helen over 25 words.

HORACE MANN ELEMENTARY SCHOOL

HELEN GETS AN EDUCATION

Helen began taking classes in speech in 1890 at Boston's Horace Mann School, a special school for the deaf. Over the course of her lifetime, it took Helen over twenty years to learn to speak so that other people could understand what she was saying.

After her schooling in Boston, she then went on to the Wright-Humason School in New York.

MARK TWAIN

At this special school for deaf students, she studied regular subjects and kept working on her speaking skills.

Helen had a passion for learning and at the age of sixteen she began to think that she would like to attend college. She went to a college prep school to get ready for college. Now that she had accomplished so much, her story had become famous. Many influential men and women were interested in meeting this young girl who had worked so hard to become educated despite her inability to see or hear.

One of the people who met Helen was the famous writer Mark Twain. Twain was amazed by this incredible young woman and decided to introduce her to one of his friends, a wealthy oil businessman by the name of Henry H. Rogers. Rogers was just as impressed by Helen as Twain was. He was in awe of her drive, persistence, determination, and talent.

HENRY H. ROGERS

RADCLIFFE COLLEGE

He agreed to sponsor her and pay for her to attend an excellent school—Radcliffe College. In order for her to attend school, she needed someone to help her understand the lectures as well as the textbooks. Anne came to school with her and helped her with all of her studies.

BRAILLE

HELEN'S BOOK

By the time she was in her last few years of college, Helen had mastered reading what people said by touching their lips. She had also become proficient at Braille, a way that blind people can read by touching raised dots on a page. She was talking so others could understand her and spelling using her fingers, as she had done with Anne.

Working with Anne and Anne's fiancé, John Macy, Helen authored her first book called, The Story of My Life. The book told about the transformation she had made from her early childhood to her college student years. Helen graduated with honors from Radcliffe when she was 24 years old.

HELEN KELLER WITH ANNE SULLIVAN MACY
AND JOHN MACY

HELEN GRADUATES FROM COLLEGE

After she graduated from college, Helen went on a quest to help others with disabilities improve their lives. She went on speaking tours and shared the experiences she had had with audiences to develop awareness of the lives of those who are blind and deaf. She co-founded an organization called Helen Keller International with George Kessler, a famous city planner. Together they worked tirelessly to fight for those who were blind or suffering from malnutrition.

She helped to establish the American Civil Liberties Union, which still fights for the individual rights of all Americans today. The American Federation for the Blind was founded in 1921 and Helen became a member. She helped raise money for their cause.

HELEN KELLER WITH POLLY THOMSON

HELEN AND ANNE'S LEGACY

Helen's beloved miracle worker died in 1936. She had been in poor health for a long time and became blind for the last four years of her life. Polly Thomson, who had worked for Helen and Anne became Helen's helper and took over Anne's duties.

Helen's and Anne's story was made into an inspiring movie in 1962 with Helen's part acted by Patty Duke and Anne's played by Anne Bancroft. Through the movie, many more people found out about her amazing journey working with Anne as she learned to communicate.

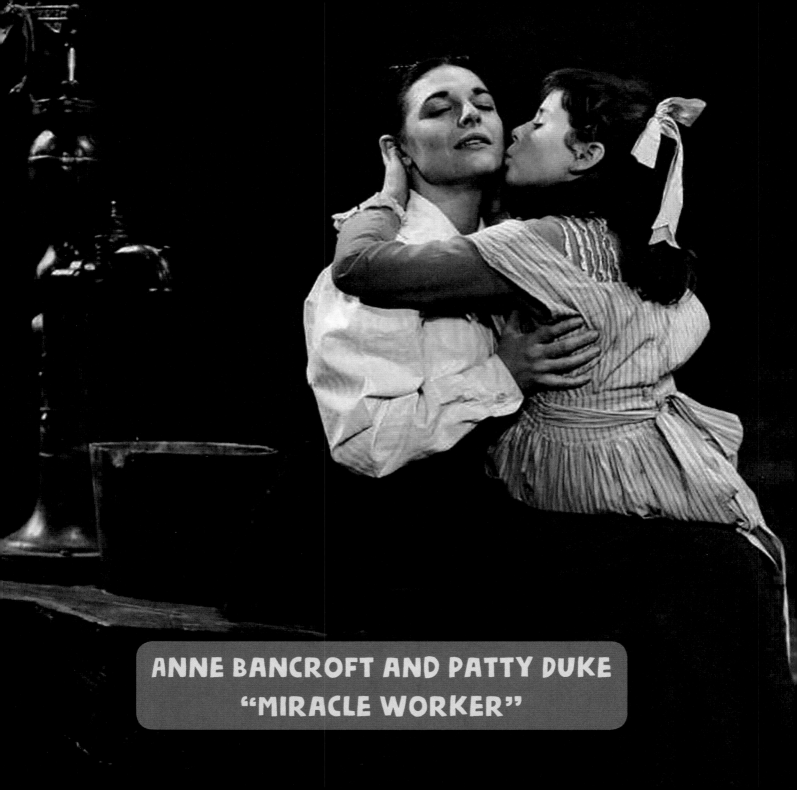

ANNE BANCROFT AND PATTY DUKE
"MIRACLE WORKER"

PRESIDENTIAL MEDAL OF FREEDOM

During her life, Helen received many awards for her efforts in helping people around the world. She was very proud of the Presidential Medal of Freedom she received in 1964.

Helen died in her sleep a few weeks before her birthday. She would have been 88 years old. Thanks to her miracle worker, Anne, and her own remarkable efforts she became known worldwide for the work she did to help others attain a better quality of life. She truly proved that no matter what obstacles you have in life, you can succeed.

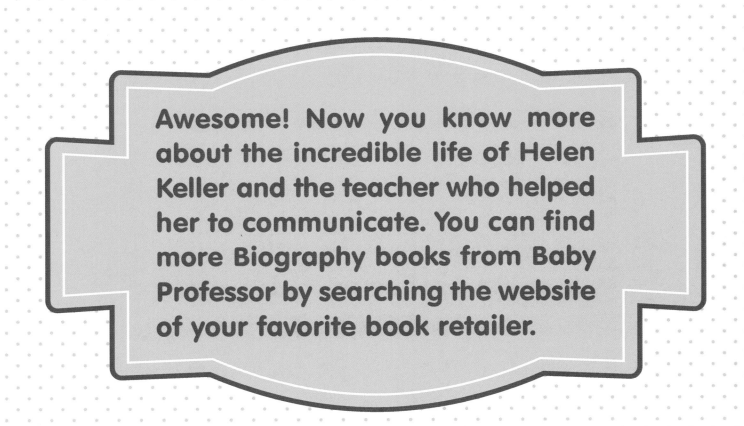

Awesome! Now you know more about the incredible life of Helen Keller and the teacher who helped her to communicate. You can find more Biography books from Baby Professor by searching the website of your favorite book retailer.